You're F*cking Welcome

You're F*cking Welcome

Copyright © 2020 by Jay Syrah for Goodwin Publishing

All rights reserved. Except for use in any review, the reproduction or utilization of this work in whole or in part in any form by any electronic, mechanical or other means, now know or hereinafter invented, including zerography, photocopying and recording, or in any information storage or retrieval system, is forbidden without permission of the publisher.

ISBN - 978-1-7363346-0-7 (paperback)

ISBN - 978-1-7363346-1-4 (ebook)

*For the next generation of rising stars.
Here's your road guide, but always
remember to forge your own path.*

Table of Contents

Introduction 1

Chapter One: Find Your Why 9

Chapter Two: Build your Foundation 17

Chapter Three: Specialize and Diversify 41

Chapter Four: Be Adaptable 47

Chapter Five: Be of Service - Job Security 57

Chapter Six: It's Who You Know 67

Chapter seven: Keep Moving 77

Chapter Eight: Raise The Stakes 85

Chapter Nine: Remember your Why 99

Closing Remarks 105

Acknowledgements 107

Introduction

During my career as a hospitality professional , It has been definitely trying. There are many ups and downs, not really knowing how to navigate from different industry segments to promotions to properties to different avenues one can take in hospitality, or further one's career. The purpose of me writing this book is to lend a helping hand. You know, for that front desk agent or that person who's promoting parties or who's becoming an event planner or a wedding planner or someone who is keenly interested in joining the hospitality industry. This is their stepping stone or better yet their "How To Guide" to get the most out of a career in the hospitality industry.

When I started my career I wish I had this tool, because I would be a lot further in my career and would have advanced quicker than where I have been. Not to take lightly, the enjoyment and the adventure that it has been, but having a planned out strategic guide would have definitely helped me a lot, when it comes to maneuvering within this industry.

So this is for all of those students in college, all of those teenagers or entry level candidates, that's looking to move up in the industry and to really create a name for themselves. This book is for you. Anybody that's ever wanted to throw a party, wanted to be a host or wanted to be a chef or restauranteur developer, travel agent etc. May it be in sports, recreation, theme parks, casinos, lodging, hotels, and anything that has to do with hospitality. This is for you guys, this is your *"How To Guide"* to get the most out of this industry.

The first thing that we're going to touch on is *"finding your why."* That is going to set you on your path and your purpose. Whatever it is that sets your soul on fire, that, is going to keep you going. So, the first and most important part is finding your why.

Then you want to *"build your foundation."* Meaning the building blocks that you will use to set up your career. This will include lessons, education, experiences, and characteristics that you will call upon when making a name for yourself.

Once you have built your foundation you will need to focus your effort, what I like to call *"specialize and diversify."* Do you want to hone in on your niche or you want to keep it broad? Whatever you do, you have to do a lot of it. For me, I focused on Food and Beverage, but I started in hotels as a front desk agent. I wanted to encompass everything that I can do within the restaurant sector. If you want to do hotels, you have to focus on everything you want to do within the hotel sector, you have to know everything.

This industry changes at the drop of a dime meaning "***being adaptable***" is key. I know from personal experience, that things are never consistent, the same things that were getting you through the last month may not carry you through the next month because this industry changes so quickly and so rapidly.

You have to stay ahead of the game and you always have to be ahead of the curve, and you have to constantly be adapting, that is one of the key traits of a hospitality professional. At any given moment things can go from, we have to host this party for 1000 people. Then boom the party planners will call and now instead of 1000 it will be 2000 people. You have to figure out how to make those things work and be adaptable. Do not let it get to you, keep a level head and then roll with the punches.

The biggest part of hospitality at its core, is to "***be of service***," which will also be your job security. You have to want to be of service. That's why we're in this industry. That is the whole purpose of this industry to be of service. You are at the beck and call and will of every guest that you encounter, every guest at a restaurant. Every patron that comes into your bar, every guest that sits down at a slot machine, rolls at a craps table, every guest that checks into a hotel. You are at their beck and call. Your job is to make their time enjoyable, that is the point of the hospitality industry, you are being of service to someone else, that is your job, that is what you are here to do! You have to get joy out of doing that! In doing that, you secure your position and future.

When you're knowledgeable, you have a solid network, you found your why coupled with your mindset of being hospitable, that secures your job. You have to do things that others aren't willing to do. Nobody technically wants to serve other people, as a job, but if you're thinking about being in this industry? That's pretty much the gist of your job in every aspect, no matter whether it's behind the scenes handling finances or you're front of house on the floor, interacting with guests. Your job is to be of service.

Putting in the work is just the tip of the iceberg , you have to apply the knowledge you gain but it's not always about what you know but what you can prove. Or in this case, *"it's who you know"* , you can have all the accreditations in the world but if you can't prove that you have this knowledge or have someone attest to the fact that you know what you're talking about and know what you're doing It's just gonna fall to the wayside. Then all you have is a piece of paper, or a pin or metal that says, Oh, I took a class that he/she is accredited in this subject, but if you can't prove it. It means nothing.

If you don't have the right people in your corner. It's just gonna be a lot of hard work, a lot of trial and error, you need to find yourself a mentor, you need to have a team of people backing you to vouch for you and validate your work to others. Keep your networking skills tight, and always look for those new opportunities because some of the best opportunities will come from your network, from your mentors, from your colleagues from people that you have worked with previously. These are the people that can attest to your work. So, always keep your game tight and always keep your network expanding. Keep your network broad and always have someone in your circle, at least two or three people in your circle that has done or is doing exactly what you want to do.

Once you have established these sets of skills and a solid network, then you're going to "***keep moving***." You never want to stay in a single place for too long. Once you feel like you learned everything you can do in a certain area, a certain location, a certain property, then it's time to move on to keep your growth growing. You have to be constantly gaining new experiences.

Do not make moves for the sake of making moves there needs to be a purpose/reason behind each move that you make, it's kind of like playing spades. Nobody knows why you are making these moves, while you're making them but, every card that you play has to have a purpose. Only you can see your hand, only you know what you're capable of and what you want to do. Only you know your end goal and only you know what your why is. So, you have to make your next move your best move.

With making your next move comes the fun part, playing the game the way it's supposed to be played. Because this industry is not for the faint of heart. It is not easy. It's not the most lucrative, but you can definitely make good money. So when you play the game you have to **"raise the stakes"**. You have to set and accomplish these goals you have to set high goals for yourself.

You have to know your worth ,and never settle. What you get out of it has to be way more than what you'll lose from it. Sometimes instead of chasing dollars, chase knowledge, chase the lessons and chase the experiences. Chase, those opportunities and the placements. That's what you want to chase in this industry, because the more experiences you have, the more knowledge you have, the better your wisdom, and the easier it will be for you to maneuver into your next step.

Lastly to bring it full circle in the last chapter, **"never forget your why"**, and do your own thing. If you really want to go substantially far in this industry, you can never forget your why. Never forget what motivated you to get into this industry in the first place. Never forget your purpose for joining this industry. Your why is what's going to keep you grounded like your root chakra.

That's going to keep your foundation solid, and that's going to keep you moving and growing in the right direction. Once you hit a certain point you will feel as though and you say to yourself "I plateaued", " I've hit my peak here". That's when you have to branch out, and you have to take everything that you learned in your entire career, then go build something for yourself. That's how you last in this industry. That's how you get the most out of this industry. That is how you will be able to impact this industry like nobody else will.

So without further ado, let's get into chapter one, which is finding your why, locating your purpose, and I hope you enjoy reading "**_You're fucking welcome_**."

CHAPTER ONE

Find Your Why

"Clarify your purpose. What is the why behind everything you do? When we know this in life or design it is very empowering and the path is clear." - Jack Canfield

When I say finding your why. That isn't about your motivation for financial gain and things like that, it's your purpose for joining this amazing industry that we call hospitality. Some people think of financial gain or think that it's a great industry to get into or the job security in it, or just looking to experience something different.

What you have to do is sit down, think to yourself, write it out, whatever you have to do, to figure out your why. Figure out what it is that is going to keep you driven, in order to succeed in this industry. From my personal experience, I will definitely let you know it's not all the glitz and glamour that is cracked up to be. Yes, you can have a lot of fun in this industry, yes, there's a lot of partying involved. Yes, there's great food, there's great drinks, there's a lot of different avenues that you can take, there's traveling, lots of celebrities and big figures and money to be made in this industry. But in my full honest opinion, if that's the only reason for getting into this industry it is not going to pan out for you. You're going to lose that passion, you're going to lose that drive, you're going to lose that desire.

So that's why the first thing you have to do is find your why. Sit down to yourself, and think of the big picture. At the end of your career or at the end of your time in the hospitality industry, What is it that you wish to accomplish? Who do you wish to inspire? What are your goals for the industry? What is it that you're looking to learn? What do you wish to accomplish when setting this goal for yourself? You really have to think about it, like it can't be like, "you know what, this seems fun. I'm gonna do it." That's a great entry point, but I'm telling you, once you get into the nitty gritty of the hospitality industry, it will chew you up and spit you out.

This industry is not for the weak of heart. This is not for those who think that this industry is a breeze to work in. There's plenty of days where you're going to want to quit. There's going to be days when you're going to question yourself, "like why did I even sign up for this?", "This is not what I thought it was." You're really going to want to give up on those days. You're going to feel like you're going insane because you might feel like you're spinning your wheels.

Your purpose brings you back to your rationale as to why you've invested this time to get into this industry. That will keep you going. That will be your motivation, that will be your drive.

You really have to focus on your why. Whether you sit down and have it on your vision board or you converse with a couple of your classmates or your family or it's part of your family business. It could be A single experience that you had while flying on a plane and the flight attendant may have given you an extra bottle to drink or didn't charge you for those cookies or those juices. You might have gotten a complimentary upgrade when you checked into your hotel one evening, when the front desk agent really took care of you and your family. There might have been a special occasion when it could've been a birthday or anniversary. Something like that left a positive memory that you have associated with this industry that made you say,"you know what, I want to be that person, I want to do what it is that they're doing, I want to do that."

It was like that for me. Honestly I wanted to impact the world. I wanted to change the world. I'm gonna be 100% honest, that was my rationale behind getting into this industry.

(Back Story)I want to say either 2000, 2001(I may be mixing up the years), I remember I'm sitting at home watching MTV and on MTV was Diddy's all white party, and I'm just looking at all this as a kid. I didn't know this is what being an adult was about and I saw everybody dressed to the nines in their all white, drinking champagne, all types of drinks and everybody's just having a good time. I mean all types of things, performers, beautiful people, exotic animals you know, lavish exuberance and all types of spectacles and people having a genuine good time. I saw that. And ,"I said, that's what I want to do!" I'd had no clue what it was, I had no clue how to get there. I was like you know what I want to be that person, I want to be Diddy, I want to be the one who throws parties like that. I wanted to be that person. And that's what initially got me into hospitality that's what piqued my interest. Not knowing it was actually the man behind the scenes that was making it happen Maneesh K. Goyal (Look him up). I didn't know the professional term was hospitality. What I knew was, I wanted to see that look on people's faces every time they came to one of my events or one of my parties. I wanted them to feel that joy, that fun that excitement, you know? I wanted them to experience that with me and I wanted to create those moments for people.

So that was my first little take on the hospitality industry, fast forward a couple years later I found myself inspired to cook. I wanted to be one of the best cooks, I wanted to be a top chef. At This time I found out what the Food Network was and the Cooking channel, it was something new to me, and it really sparked my interest and my dad would always barbecue and I found out I could make really good food. (well I was decent at grilling) And that's another stepping stone for me that ultimately led me to being in hospitality. And then in high school I let go of the hospitality thing for a little while. I was focused on automotive technology. Then I started to go to parties. You know the average teenager in high school,you started going to parties. And once again, I was hit with that bug at one of the parties, it was a sweet 16 I was noticing everybody having so much fun. I realized again my why, "Yo, this is what I want to do, like, I want to throw parties I want to promote parties!" once again had no way of knowing how to get there. All I knew was it was something I wanted to do. So I ditched my aspects of wanting to be in the automotive industry.

As soon as I graduated high school, I found myself in community college majoring in business because I knew I wanted to own restaurants and nightclubs. That's what I wanted to do. I'm in community college, focusing on a business major, and lo and behold, I'm with one of my college friends Desia (thank you Desia), and she tells me about this class that she's taking that I should join in the second semester. She said, "Look, I hear you keep saying how you want to promote and you want to do nightclubs and you want to do restaurants. Why don't you take this class with me, because it's exactly what you want to do?" I was Like what is it called, she said, "***hospitality***." And from that point forward. I was able to give a name to what I wanted to do.

I was able to focus on exactly what it is I wanted to do and the industry I wanted to be in. Fast forward two years later I found myself at the University of North Carolina Greensboro, and I'm fully immersed in the whole hospitality industry. I landed my first job at a hotel at one of the, the number one hotels in Greensboro. I had the pleasure of actually working for the top one, and top two hotels in Greensboro, The O'henry & Proximity hotels. But the way I knew that I was meant to be in this industry was, as soon as I got to Greensboro, the first thing I did as a college student, you know, looking to support myself and branch out. I started looking for a job. Within a week of being in Greensboro, I secured five interviews with three callbacks, and two job offers. I ended up making a decision to not go the major corporate route, and not go with the name brand company, instead I went for the independently owned, locally operated company that held more prestige and more notoriety. From doing that I set a standard for myself.

I set a standard for myself, that once you reach this level, you can only go up from here. From there I ended up being in various jobs titles. I started to hone my skills, and it always came back to my "why" I wanted to provide a feeling. I wanted to provide a memory of a story. I wanted to be a part of that storytelling. That, "I remember when I went here to do this and I did this, and he helped me do it. I was the facilitator of these emotions linked to these memories and of these feelings of joy, happiness, excitement. I was the facilitator and that brought me joy, bringing other people joy.

That was my "why" that I found at a young age. Never did I realize it was going to take me through so many different avenues and so many different paths, throughout all my ups and downs, all of my trials and tribulations. I had to focus on my "Why". Why was I doing this? I wanted to change people's lives. I wanted to impact people's lives in a positive way, a lasting memory. Up to this point I would definitely say that I accomplished my goal.

I definitely have a lot further to go to. I learned that you have to keep going, never stop where you are, it's always a new height to reach, a new level to go to. So you always gotta keep going. And that's one of the things that I've learned in finding and chasing my "Why". Always chase your "why", money will come, experiences will come, some good, some bad, but your "why" should never change, it should only expand. Your "why" is going to keep you driven, your "Why" is going to keep you motivated, your "why" is going to keep you grounded.

perfect wall. An unshakable foundation, on what you can build upon that, will not falter or crumble under stress. So that is the basis of this chapter, building your foundation in the hospitality industry consisting of a few concepts or traits.

* 11 Traits of a Hospitality Professional*

The first bricks are a set of characteristics. You want to hone these skills and you want to build these skills. In my opinion there are 11 major characteristics that are found in every hospitality professional. Now this list is not limited to or the end all be all because I am pretty sure there's a lot of attributes and characteristics that I'm missing in this list, but we're going to go through 11. These are the most influential traits that one should possess. Now these are not numbered in any specific order by scale of greatness, but these are very very important when you set off into your hospitality endeavor. Then we will jump into the types of education that one should possess starting with formal education, then education from experience, and then we will close with the experience from others. They differ in specific ways, two of which, you're going to get hands on while the last one is basically a mentor or someone sharing with you, what they've come to learn in their time of being a hospitality professional.

We're going to go ahead and jump right into the 11 characteristics of a hospitality professional.

CHAPTER TWO

Build your Foundation

> *"You don't set out to build a wall. You don't say "I'm going to build the biggest, baddest, greatest wall that's ever been built." you don't start there. You say," I'm going to lay this brick as perfectly as a brick can be laid. You do that every day. And soon you will have a wall."* - WILL SMITH

Once you have your "Why" established and defined, the next thing is to hit the ground running. I want to start off with a story told by the great Will Smith on how building foundations are key to longevity in any industry and any objective and goal. You want to start with a strong, stable foundation. Will Smith and his brother were propositioned by his father to rebuild a wall. The caveat was that they had to lay one brick each day as perfect, as straight and as neat as they possibly could. Yes, it would have taken a long time. Yes it was tedious, but at the end of the process you had a

So that is my test for you before you even continue to read this book before you even consider the pathway that you want to go. Whether it be the food and beverage industry, the hotel industry, the nightclub industry, the bar industry or the travel industry, recreational industry, agriculture, lodging, games and casino industry. Everything that you focus on, every decision that you make will have your "why" behind it, because if it doesn't have your why behind it, you're going to lose sight of the goal.

Positive Energy

The first being *__positive energy__*. Positive energy is key in this industry, because you're going to be combated with so much negativity, from things not going as they should to all types of conundrums, problems and different trials and adversities that you're going to have to overcome. Positive energy would definitely keep you going. Positive energy is contagious, positive energy will definitely outshine negative energy in all aspects.

Generally speaking, having positive energy is key to anything in life, because it shows through the law of attraction when you have negative energy and you possess negative thoughts they compound bringing towards you manifestations that which you think of consistently. So you want to be consistently positive, be persistently positive, and you want to embody positivity. It will bring to you so much good fortune, so many great occurrences, spontaneity and manifestations that will just make you love and continue to thrive in this industry.

Positive energy affects not only you, but those around you. Say you have someone coming in and their flight might have been delayed or their order was wrong, or, they misplaced their tickets or what have you, and you're the first person, they come in contact with after said mishaps. It won't be your fault at all, but you're going to catch the brunt of that, you're going to catch all that negative energy, you're going to catch all that hostility. Because you know what, you're there and they have to vent to you. You have to remain calm and remain positive because your positive energy can disarm negative energy. You have to transfer your positive energy to get them into a positive mood. If you combat negativity with negativity, you're just gonna end up in this big shouting match, you're gonna end up with a terrible experience. You're gonna end up with a headache.

At the end of the day, and at the rate of how many people and how many guests that you may frequent in a single day, it just works out better to be positive. If you focus on too many negative things you're gonna have so much negative energy, and your day is just gonna go down the shiter. I promise you that I know this from experience, and it's just a hell of a lot better just to be positive, all around. You'll see you'll be a lot happier, you'll make better memories and people will gravitate to you more. It's just better to be around a positive person. Nobody wants to be around a negative Nancy all the time. She's just fucking depressing. Nobody *wants* to be depressed. Nobody *wants* to be a Debbie downer. Right? So that's the first and foremost thing that you want to have when coming into hospitality you want to be the positive one. You want to be the one that's always in a good mood (on stage at least). You want to be the one that always has high energy that's always down for you know, a good time.

YOU'RE F*CKING WELCOME

Generosity

The second trait you want to have is **generosity**. A lot of times you'll find yourself, giving. That's pretty much what hospitality is, you give of yourself, you give a good, you give services. You have to be generous when you give, and you have to give with an open heart. Because, once again, you are facilitating. You are the facilitator of great memories. So be generous with your time, be generous with your services. Be generous, when you're speaking. Be generous with information, help somebody out. This goes with colleagues as well.

When you see someone struggling, be generous, help somebody out. Help them lift those packages, if you see someone is struggling with a negative guest, be generous, step in and intervene. You could easily just look the other way. You never know how that generosity might come back to you. It's better to give than receive, and that is a point in this industry, you're going to be giving a lot, you're going to be giving away products, you're going to be giving away a lot of your free time, you're going to be giving away a lot of yourself. So you have to be able to give, and that ties into positive energy. Who gives angrily? That leads to resentment. Right? It does. Have you ever seen somebody give angrily? That means they shouldn't be giving in the first place. Right? Then the person that's doing the receiving is reluctant to actually take what has been given, because at that point is like here! This all I can do for you get the fuck out my face. Right? So you want to be positive, and you want to be generous in the same aspect.

Be Friendly

The third characteristic is that you want to be *friendly*. You have to be friendly, because you'll meet a lot of people, actually countless people day in and day out. In the course of a day you might see hundreds of people. So you have to keep that approachable demeanor that I'm here to help you attitude. You have to be a friend to complete strangers that you might not see again. If you play your cards right, they'll become your regulars. You'll get to know these people then you get to build a relationship with them. Nobody wants to be friends with a miser or someone with a mean disposition. Friendliness will definitely help you in the long run. You'll be way more agreeable, you'll have more friends, better connections, and genuine relationships. When you're friendly, it makes it easier for people to come to you when you get into management positions or leadership roles. You're a lot easier to relate to when you're friendly, because you're not seen as distant or off putting, then you are seen as a go to person. Your name will move in circles as the person that if there's ever any troubles, you will be a goto.

Solution Oriented

Number four, characteristic of a hospitality professional is to be *solution oriented*, you want to be a critical thinker, you want to have great critical thinking skills. Time and time again, you will use them to solve problems. You will never know how many decisions you have to make, or what chain reaction may occur until shit hits the fan. When a problem occurs, you have to be able to make a quick decision and not just make a quick decision but make an informed and educated decision.

There's been times when I personally had to figure out things on my own. In a very short time, whether it be reservations being overbooked. Running out of a certain supply or product, you have to figure out where you can get this. What's the next best solution because your initial solution is not available. You have to think who can I go to to get this? Who do I know that has what that I need or what is the best alternative? What other solution can I provide other than the one that I originally wanted to employ? You have to do it in a timely manner, because the longer it takes for you to make a decision or produce a solution the worse things get. From the guest perspective, 30 seconds at a dining room table will seem like an eternity. Especially when you're waiting for something, or when a problem is going on. Trust me. I've seen both sides, from being a patron, waiting for something to be corrected, to being the one that has to do the corrections. The longer you take the worse the situation gets. You just have to come up with a solution. Even if you come up with a solution that buys you time, a solution is a solution. Postpone the actual solution, do what you have to do to off put the negativity, to provide some type of compensation or correction. You have to think quickly, and your judgment has to be there. And you have to be effective in your thinking.

Lead By Example

The number five characteristics is to **lead by example**. You definitely have to be an example. You have to be a leader. That's going to set you apart. Leading by example is doing what others won't do or doing what is against the grain to get the job done. Your willingness to do whatever it takes and whatever you have to do to get whatever needs to be done. If you have a team of people who feel negatively about a certain situation or a certain task, and you know that if this doesn't get done, the whole team fails. You have to be the first one to step out there. You have to be the one to lead your people, that separates leaders from managers. Managers will just tell you what to do and bark orders at you, leaders will actually show you how to do it, show you how to get ahead. Leaders provide demonstrations, and they will essentially hold your hand and walk you through it, so that the next time, you'll know exactly what to do. Lead by example set the trend, set the new standard. Setting the new precedent being that example you wish you had. Then watch, watch how your respect grows, watch how your admiration grows. You end up being the one that can be depended on, you'll get called up because they know you to be this person who is a born leader, this person who goes above and beyond. He or she is known to get the job done. That starts by leading by example.

Keep An Open Mind

In leading by example you have to be amenable to the ideas of others which leads us to the sixth characteristic: ***keeping an open mind***. Keep an open mind because this industry is very confrontational. You never know what somebody's going through. You never know what cultural differences one may have. You never know what may have happened prior to you getting into a situation or prior to this person getting to you. Something that I have experienced in my time in the hospitality industry is, there are definitely cultural differences and differences of opinion because hospitality encompasses the entire world. It's a melting pot of multiple cultures coming together as one. If you're close minded, you're just going to have confrontation after confrontation. You have to be open minded in your understanding too.

You have to be open minded to explore new possibilities. The way that you're used to thinking, or the way that you're used to doing something might not be efficient, it might not work the best for a given situation. You have to be open to new alternatives, you have to be open to different points of views, you have to be open to different ways of thinking. and not only be open to it but then encompass it into your own repertoire of useful tactics, useful thinking,and your methods. You have to be able to utilize, respect and adapt to what you're not normally used to. You have to think this is not what I was taught, but it makes sense. Let me try it out, if it works, it works if it doesn't, stick to your guns. If it does, you learned something new. It might save you a bunch of time. You might have made a new relationship or a new connection, just by keeping an open mind. I found that when I keep an open mind, it allows me to relate to people, people that I would never relate to , or give the time of day to talk to outside of the establishment where I work.

People are waiting just to socialize with open minded people and hearing different stories. You know, hearing both sides of the story and not judging people based on their culture or based on the way they think because everybody's entitled to their own thinking. Everyone is brought up differently, no two people were brought up the same. It might be commonalities, but no two people were ever brought up the same.

So you have to be open minded. You have to be respectable. And you have to be able to tolerate differences of opinions. Because there's going to be a lot of people that are going to try to get under your skin by forcing their opinions on you. They're going to try to force their point of view, they're gonna try to shove it down your throat. It's not that they're right and it's not that they're wrong, but they just want to be heard, and at the same time, you want to get your point across. You have to be open minded and respect that they also have an opinion.

Adaptability

That leads us to the number seven characteristic **adaptability.** You have to be able to adapt. This industry changes so rapidly, more rapidly than one would think. Every season, there's a new fad coming out, there's a new product, there's a new hot thing, there's a new craze that hits the streets. When it hits the industry, then everybody is looking to get on. Being adaptable keeps you ahead of the game, it allows you to continue to ride the waves. Even though it's better to create these waves, from a business standpoint. Be able to ride these waves and know when a wave is ending and then catch the next one, and the next one. You have to be able to adapt to these conditions, dynamics and these procedures that change constantly.

Just because you're used to doing things a certain way, does not mean they can't change. Things change all the time. It's kind of like philosophy.I believe the saying goes."Today's reality is not tomorrow's future." Something along those lines. with that you have to be constantly adapting, you have to be engaged, you have to be in the know. You always gotta be looking at the next best thing, you always got to see what works and what doesn't work. You got to keep it moving. You got to keep up with the times, you got to keep up with the technology, you got to keep up with the new hot trends, the fads, the differences in procedures and how things get done. You have to be adaptable and not only in the industry as a whole but in your day to day operations.

There have been countless times when I've interacted with meeting planners and wedding planners. Even with my bosses for instance when it came to dinner reservations, when it came to occupancy or when it came to VIPs. A lot of these things you can't prepare for, a lot of these things are going to throw you for a loop, a lot of these things are going to come from left field. You have to be able to adapt to circumstances, even if you're not prepared for it. You have to be able to maneuver quickly. You have to be able to switch directions at the drop of a dime, because things are always changing. And if you're able to change with it at the same rate , you will do great in this industry.

Hard Work Ethic

They say that hard work produces results. The eighth trait and something that everyone should definitely possess is a **hard work ethic.** You want to be hard working and hard work pays off. No matter what anyone says. Mentally, or physically, hard work pays off but you have to put the work in. You only get out what you put into this industry. If you put in hard work, if you put in blood, sweat and tears if you put in the overtime, I promise you it will pay off. It might not pay off in the manner in which you expect it to. But I promise you, hard work, always pays off.

Don't let anybody tell you take the easy route, or that you're working too hard. Don't listen to the naysayers, don't listen to the lazy ones. Don't listen to the people that're trying to take the shortcuts. When you take shortcuts, you end up having to do the same work twice. You never want to do the same thing twice. Do it right the first time and do it to the best of your ability. It will save you time and your work will show that you took the time and effort to do it right. It's not to say that there's not an easier way of doing something, but it's about doing it right, and doing it to the best of your ability. It goes back to laying that single brick as perfectly as you possibly can. That is hard work, it's tedious, and it's time consuming, but once you lay that brick the best you can that wall you have built, that foundation you have built will be unshakable, it will be so perfect that your work will be revered, and it will be praised.

Hard work pays off. Once word gets that you work hard, people start to take notice. Hard working people appreciate hard work, and then, you start getting called up for new opportunities because they know that you work hard, and you give it your all and you do it to the best of your ability. Countless times in my career people will tell me, "you know you're doing too much, You're working too hard just let it go like have somebody else do that." No, let me work hard, because when it's my passion, I enjoy working hard, and I know the rewards that I get out of it. It's going to be way better than me taking the easy route. Like I said earlier, you are going to do the same work twice. It's like the old carpentry saying goes. Measure twice, cut once. If you do it right the first time you won't have to repeat it. But if you decide let me just measure once with the thought of, "there that seems about right to draw the line there" and cut it. You go to put up drywall or framing come to find out you're off by inch. Why are you off by an inch? You failed to measure twice. You failed to do your job, and you took the easy way out. So number eight is about hard work, hard work pays off, put in the work, get the rewards. I promise you you will not regret it.

Empathy

The ninth characteristic is **empathy.** Which is something I had to learn. it's not necessarily taking credit or taking the blame for things that go wrong. It's not letting it get worse. That is the best way I can describe it. Empathy is not letting a bad situation get worse and being understanding of someone else's bad situation. Even though it might not be your fault and might not have nothing to do with it, but because they brought it to your doorstep. You have to feel for them. You have to understand what emotions they're going through, how they feel, and acknowledge that. You have to say "You know what I understand about your situation. Trust me, I would feel the same way. For that, let me do this for you.", "This is what we can do to move forward." How about we move in this direction to bring back the positivity. How about we do this or that, empathy will save so many interactions. You have to understand that, especially in hospitality. It will be countless times when you will use this trait. Invest in using it in your everyday life when something goes wrong. When you have a bad interaction, or even with friends, when they come to you venting or with your family issues or what have you. Guests will bring you something that has nothing to do with you, But they brought it to you because you're the one they see. It's nothing personal. It's nothing you did, but you're about to catch the butt of it because you're the last person they see so you have to be empathetic, you have to be understanding, feel what they're feeling. It's your job as a hospitality professional to make it right. It doesn't have to be a grand gesture, it doesn't have to be something outlandish or super off the wall. Something simple will fix a lot of problems, and you won't even realize, and a simple acknowledgement of what they're going through could mean the world to somebody. I promise you that you will see the change in their demeanor, in their tone and in their posture and in their body language. Practice empathy. Master this skill for it will come in handy down the road.

Love

Characteristic Number 10 is *love.* Operate out of love. Love what you do. Love ties back into that positive energy. When you operate out of love, You bring yourself good things. They just gravitate to you. You want to do good things, you want to be positive, you want to be generous, you want to be friendly, you want to be empathetic. All of these things tie into love, and love will keep you going. Love will have you wanting to get that person that late check out because you know it's their anniversary. You want to love what you do, and love the people around you and love your team. Love can be encompassed into so many aspects of your entire hospitality career. Act out of love, show love, and love will be returned to you. It's a full circle of giving and taking, and it just keeps going. It's the gift that never stops giving, you get love here you'll give love here, you get love there you'll get love here. It's one of those things that you just have to have hands down. It's overlooked and is not thought about as much, But love honestly will keep you in a lot of places, it will open a lot of doors. And it will provide so many great experiences and turnaround so many things for you.

Love is the driving force. So use that as your power. When it comes to difficult situations, or with something as simple as I don't want to get up this morning to go to work. Remember that when you love what you do it's not technically work for you. It's fun. You want to do it, you want to be able to provide that service. You want to be of service to those with whom you come in contact. When you love what you do you will never work a day in your life. That is very true. There have been plenty of days when I just woke up feeling great, saying I just love what I do. At that point the hard work doesn't seem as hard. It seems easy. A lot of people in my profession, a lot of my colleagues who don't have the same passion and the drive for this industry, won't get it. They'll be confused, they'll be baffled at this, so I had to break it down like, "Look this is what I love to do, So I'm gonna do everything I can in this industry. I'm gonna be happy and I'm gonna do it with a smile on my face." There's been plenty of days when I will wake up, not wanting to go to work or not wanting to, you know, come in that day. Then I walk through those doors and that love, when I get there hits different because on a consistent basis you give love. Right? So on a consistent basis if you give love, when you walk into that building. When you clock in, or when you see your colleagues or coworkers, that regular guest that comes in all the time, and they give you love. It makes you feel good. They bring you new people, and then you get to show love to new people and you get some new love. You get introduced to new people because you operate out of love, and it will boost your spirits. You don't even realize how much it'll boost your spirits. It'll bring you out of a dark place, And it'll make everything worthwhile.

Thick Skinned

Last but not least, one of the most important traits, in my opinion, if not the most important trait is you got to be **thick skinned**. There's been so many times when I wanted to quit. It's been so many times when I just wanted to curse somebody out. This is a tough industry like I said. You'll get called all types of names, talked down to , called all types outlandish, slanderous,derogatory things. If you don't have thick skin or if you're not tough enough to endure those things and take that negative energy and turn it into a positive, you will not last in this industry. This industry will chew you up and spit you out. I promise you this. It is not easy, but when you know how to handle it. When you know it's really nothing personal….sometimes. You're going to last. You'll be able to maneuver. You'll be able to get over it. You won't take it personally and you'll get to the root of what the problem is, just solve the problem a lot quicker. When you're thick skinned, because now you're thinking with a level head, now you're not thinking with or acting on emotions. You're acting on solving a problem. It Helps me personally, to think to myself, okay I need to get this person the fuck out my face, how do I do this the quickest way possible? If you are acting on emotions. You won't be able to do that.

So we talked about the 11 characteristics of a hospitality professional, like I said that is just a short list of key characteristics that I've come across in my, in the industry that I know have helped me in my career to make it to where I am.

Types of Education

Now we want to talk about education. We are going to focus on three sectors. The first being formal education. The second is education from experience. And then last the experience of others. So we're just going to jump right into it. With formal education.

Formal Education

Formal education refers to schooling classes, seminars, things where you sit down and are taught in a classroom environment or in a lecture or a group setting. I personally recommend this form of education. Taking classes, sitting in on lectures, attending seminars, they all pay off. I don't care if anybody tells you that you don't need these outlets, which is true you don't technically need to do these things. If you want to be the best? If you want to go far, you will do whatever you need to do and you will learn as much as you can, read newspapers, magazines, and books. I will tell you one thing about formal education from a university. It is not the end all be all, because it goes but so far. Formal education in its basic form is theory. It teaches you theory, it teaches you the basics, it tells you in an educational way trends based on the past. It basically prepares you for your experiences. This is the first portion of experience where you will definitely get your taste of the hospitality industry, and what it is to be expected.

I went to college to get my hospitality degree. I am a humble alumni of the University of North Carolina at Greensboro. I Earned my bachelor's in hospitality management, with a minor in entrepreneurship. The hospitality program was located in the business school and my university taught me the business of hospitality. I was able to be exposed to a number of different classes and courses and learn different aspects that encompass hospitality. You never realize how big hospitality is, until you start taking classes. Classes that you wouldn't even realize that would be a part of hospitality. Great example, sustainability and sports entertainment is a part of hospitality. When it comes to casinos, gaming and regulations. In the business sector, accounting, micro and macro economics are a part of hospitality because at the end of the day somebody has to keep up with the money. By always learning, building a foundation of knowledge is going to help you so much along the way. You'll have professors who are accredited who love the industry and have built a successful career and they want to pass on knowledge. That's all formal education is the passing of knowledge in a classroom setting, either in a small classroom ,a large format classroom setting or even virtually. Some come with accreditations like certificates and certifications with titles.

For example, I took a class and I became a certified wedding planner. I went to bartending school and received my bartending certification. If you want to be a wine specialist or Sommelier there's classes and certifications that you can take for that. If you want to expand your knowledge on the Gaming Commission, you can take classes on that. If you want to be a Food Handler or if you want to run restaurants there's management classes you can take. You can even be a Certified Event Specialist. There's so many different ways to learn, and classes you can take to further yourself and build a solid foundation for this hospitality industry. All it comes down to is learning. That's all it is just learning from people who are accredited and have done what you're striving to do. Once you have completed the courses you now possess the knowledge and prowess to be able to replicate and regurgitate what it is you have been taught. Formal education is a big thing and I highly recommend it. It gives you a better experience. While also giving you a basis of knowledge to work from when you go up to the second phase of education which is experience.

Hands on Experience

A lot of us actually learn better from hands-on experience. I am definitely one of them. I will say that while I was getting my bachelor's degree I definitely held a job in hospitality, all four okay five years. It was super easy and it was super beneficial for me. Yes, I missed out on a lot of things I didn't get to party as much as I would like to, but I made the most out of my experience. I was able to go to school during the day and learn about the hospitality industry.(Theory) Then in the evening, take what I learned in class and apply it to my job. (Practice) That was the best thing about it, I was taking my knowledge that I learned in school and seeing it applied in real world experiences, and it made my classes easier. Also it made how I handle my situations a hell of a lot simpler. My advice, jump Into those internships, join those clubs, get that work experience. You know, build that foundation, if learning from experiences is the brick of a foundation then formal education is the cement that holds it together. They work hand in hand, you can't have one without the other. You can't build the wall with just cement alone, you have to have the bricks, and you have to have the cement. But what brings it all together?

Experience from others

To complete the total package is experience from others, because they're the ones that are gonna teach you how to maneuver, they're the ones that're really going to pass on what it is actually going to be like in the industry. They teach you based on what they went through and even though times are changing, they will be your best bet for advice on what has worked and how things went down. They teach you what works best in given situations because there'll be plenty of situations that you'll get into and your school knowledge won't help you, and you haven't gained the proper experience yet. So it's always good to have a mentor in your corner. It's always good to have people who have done what you want to do, and have gotten to places where you want to be. They will help you navigate.

They can be anyone in the industry. Like bosses, ex-coworkers, they can even be people that you don't know. Like celebrities, people that you admire, heroes, chairman's and CEOs, or independent business owners. People that you look up to that have put in the work already. That is the best part of learning from others. They put in the work already so it's like a roadmap. That is exactly what this book is, it is a roadmap, to guide you to get the most out of this hospitality industry because someone has already done it, follow the footsteps, the path is laid out for you. Don't be hesitant to go off on your own way, to learn for yourself. Take the knowledge and apply it to your situations and apply it to what works best for you.

You want to always remember the three forms of education. You want to get formal education. Be it classes, certifications, seminars, lectures, things like that. Get accredited to show that you have this knowledge in a classroom setting. Then you want to get education from experience, which is big groundwork. It's an application of what you have learned. Putting what you learned in theory into action. It's going to be your biggest teacher, because you're going to try and fail, but never get discouraged because in order to grow you have to fail. The key is to limit those failures. The way you limit those failures is by learning from the experience of others. Having someone or having multiple people in your corner. That will be able to tell you where they messed up, where they fell short, what they wish they would have done better, or if they had been in the same shoes or in the same situation, how they wish they would have handled situations. People who have been through situations love to tell what they've been through, especially if you're in the same industry. They love to pass on the knowledge. They love to lend that helping hand.

All it takes is a quick question. "Have you been in this situation before because I'm having a tough time with it, or what would you do, what did you do when you were in this position?" How did you handle this, because I'm having difficulties. Admit that is difficult, admit that it's not easy, and ask for help.

To wrap up, laying the groundwork and building your foundation. You want to build on your characteristics the 11 characteristics of a hospitality professional. Build those experiences and that education. Those are your basic fundamentals for laying proper groundwork for making sure your foundation is stable. you will constantly be building upon this foundation. That's what foundation is, it's solid ground, and it's stability to build upon. So you're going to take all these experiences, all these characteristics, all these traits and this education, all this knowledge that you have gained. Then you're going to build upon it.

CHAPTER THREE

Specialize and Diversify

"The best investment you can make, is an investment in yourself the more you learn the more you earn" - Warren buffett

In chapter two, we talked about how you need to build your foundation. A stable foundation is greatly needed to grow yourself in the hospitality industry. What we're going to get into in this chapter is what to do after you've built your foundation and touching back to chapter one, you found your "**why**" you're going to put these two together. By this time you should have figured out what area or niche that you gravitate to the most. That's what you will specialize in, you want that to be your focus, that's the area that you want to excel in the most.

It's basically what calls to you where you feel you will have the most impact in pursuing your "why". This will be what brings you the most joy. You want to focus on that because the hospitality industry, like I said before and I'll say time and time again, will definitely take you in a lot of different avenues and many different routes. You have to be diligent and you have to take all of your energy and your efforts and focus it on a single avenue. Of course within a single avenue, there will be multiple ways of getting the goal done, that's where diversification will come into play.

First we're going to touch on the specialization. When I say specialize, you want to focus, meaning you want to focus on what drives you. For me, after I built my foundation and tested the waters in a couple places. I landed on food and beverage. That's my specialization, food and beverage. I knew that's what I wanted to do. I knew that I could accomplish the most, and I was most useful in food and beverage. So I focused on that. I spent the most time in food and beverage, whether that be event planning, serving , bartending, set-up, kitchen expo and management. That's what I challenge you to do: find your area to specialize in and want to be your area of expertise. When it comes to specializing, you want to look for a few things.

1. It has to motivate you

2. You have to feel like you're going to be able to accomplish the most in that niche

3. It has to call to your why

4. Can you expand on it?

Those are the top four determining factors that will help you figure out your niche. That's how you know you have to specialize in it. Then ,You attack! Full force, you have to give it all you got. Encompass everything about that niche, everything you do has to be about that special niche no matter the industry.

Me being in the food and beverage industry. A lot of doors opened for me. I met a lot of people. I was able to do hotels, I was able to do restaurants, I was able to do event planning, wedding planning, bars, nightclubs, things like that. And I was able to do all of these things because they are focused on a single lane within the hospitality industry. I never said I wanted to do it all. I just found out that I love food and beverage. I love great food. I mean, who doesn't love great food right? It's one of the world's universal languages. Everybody can have a good time and everybody comes together over a good meal or over great drinks. You will even see that at work at the end of a long shift in some restaurants the chef's come out and bring big hotel pans of food after service. That's for everybody, it's called family meal. It's a celebration. Let's break bread together because we got through another shift. That's what it's about it's, it's about bringing people together. That's why you got to specialize, you got to pick a lane and drive it to the best of your ability.

Now you don't have to stay in the single lane. Specialization is like a four lane highway. You technically have several different ways that you can go in the same direction. You have the fast lane, you have the passing lane, you have the slow lane and then some highways have the merging lane. So, at different areas in your career, you'll be in different lanes but it's all going to the same place it's all headed in the same direction. That's what you have to do . You gotta focus your drive on a single destination. Then at a certain point, when you feel like I don't want to be in the fast lane anymore. Get in the slow lane. Where you can take your time with it, that's when you get into diversification, it's learning everything about that significant or that specific niche that makes you diversify.

Getting back to food and beverage. I wanted to learn everything about food and beverage so I ended up taking classes on management. I learned how to control crowds, I learned fire and safety regulations. I had to learn how to do invoices, scheduling, payroll and basic accounting duties. These skills technically are outside of the food and beverage scope, but that niche cannot survive without these things so you diversify. That's what I mean by, you have to learn everything that has to do with that special niche,and be good at it.

You don't have to be the best, but you have to be well versed enough that if you're called to do that position or if you're called to handle those duties. You can handle those duties, without having to ask for help or without too much direction. It's been several times when I had to perform duties outside of my job description. I would have never guessed that I would eventually be a booking agent, because I was handling locating, booking and paying entertainment. I had to make sure they got paid and I had to make sure their schedules were right. That was a part of my niche that I didn't know I would have to do. I didn't know I would technically be an entertainment manager.

I learned everything I could within that niche. It worked out in my favor because now I can add that to my resume. Wherever I go, that little bit of time spent doing that responsibility will come in handy and help me progress further in my career. You want to diversify as best as you can. It's like being a professional poker player, but youre specialty is texas holdem'.

CHAPTER FOUR

Be Adaptable

> *"It Is not the strongest of the species that survives, nor the most intelligent that survives. It is the one that is most adaptable to change." - Charles Darwin*

To reference Charles Darwin and his studies in the Galapagos Islands, on how the animals that survived are the ones that adapted to their surroundings. The same fate can be correlated to the hospitality industry; the ones surviving are accustomed to always changing, and to things around them changing very quickly. You'll recall in chapter two. Under the 11 characteristics of a hospitality professional. The number seven trait was adaptability. Well, that trait is a lot bigger than one can give credit. In the industry of hospitality, everything is based on what's new, what's now and what's happening. It's changing almost as quickly as technology. The rule of thumb is that technology changes every year. which is true. It also can coincide with information. There's new information being given out every 18 months, something changes and you have to be either ahead of the game, or you have to be agile enough to be able to change directions, and adapt to your surroundings without hesitation.

I had to learn that several times during my career in hospitality. Sometimes it might be as early as two weeks out, something might change. It might be as late as an hour before an event starts, something will change, and the changes won't always be something little. For example the guest count changes, or a high profile special attendee coming in. It'll be a big thing. I remember one time in my events days when I was a part of the event setup team. I had to change the setup of a room at least three to five times, because every time we set up a room, someone else (authority, managers, directors, ownership) would come in and be like, "oh I don't like it! How about if we move this here? And if we move that there?" This wasn't an easy task. There was a lot of furniture involved, there were a lot of moving pieces, and it was a lot of setup. This was the day of, and it got to a point where there were too many chefs in the kitchen, or as the other saying goes, too many chiefs and no Indians. Except me and the banquet setup crew were the Indians, and it was too many chiefs, trying to dictate orders or whoever had say so over the outcome and the setup of the event space.

It will get to you if you're not thick skinned, and it will be annoying, to say the least. Literally I wanted to chop somebody's fucking head off several times. It was like, come on we did this eight times already I am tired. I worked a 12 hour shift already. Then I had to turn around, change my clothes and then work this damn event, and you can't decide on a basic setup. Like you want an extra chair here or an extra chair there. You want us to move this giant sofa, that weighs 300 fucking pounds?

You have to be able to adapt and adapt quickly, because everything is constantly changing, and you have to be a step ahead of the game. And that was just one example. Adaptability also pertains to the industry as a whole.

There's always new technology coming out, there's new gadgets to help businesses generate more revenue. A big change that happened during my career is social media. When I first started social media was something that was just getting started, you know, it was Myspace, Facebook and Twitter. That was it. Then Instagram came along, Snapchat came along, Pinterest came along. Those platforms just came along and changed the game. They changed the game for the better. Now information is able to reach the masses at a more rapid pace and it's great for marketing. It's great for business, driving revenue and exposure. Those are the types of things you have to be on top of because there's a lot of restaurants, hotels, and industries that are super late to that wave. It's like being the last one out to recess, and you only have 10 minutes left to play when you actually get 45 minutes. Like you wasted all of that time, when you could have been having fun and enjoying it. Now you have 10 minutes to try to get the most out of what you have left. That's stressful; it's also taxing knowing you missed a bunch of opportunities.

It's the same thing with trends, you have to follow trends, you have to stay ahead of the trends like its fashion. In fashion, how can you tell what's going to be hot two seasons from now? More than likely It is what you've seen in a fashion show earlier that year. New York Fashion Week will show you the styles that are coming out for the spring/summer in the fall/winter. So they show you two seasons ahead, what is going to be hot, what is going to be craved and what is going to sell. That sets the tone and you can pick up on these little traits prior to the big wave crashing and you can capitalize on it as an industry.

It's a great tool to be ahead of the game to be able to see when things are going to go a certain way. Like, I was fortunate enough to work in an open kitchen restaurant (Shoutout Green Valley Grill) meaning you can see directly into the kitchen. You can see the chefs, you can see the servers, and you can see the runners, from your table. This was years before it became hot. I mean years before it actually caught on at my next location. (No offense Cherry) I was like, we were doing that four or five years ago you guys are late. Catching the tail end of a wave does not mean you have to miss the wave. It just means that something else will pop up very soon. Like now it's the whole vegan craze. Everything is vegan; drinks, barbecue, caribbean, pizza etc. It's about being ahead of the game or even noticing trends while they're trends and capitalizing on it, making sure that you can get the most out of it, without being the last one, you know, to get the joke.

It's noticing there is something new that is going to catch on. Let's prepare ourselves, let's make these adjustments. Let us try to make the most out of what is changing right now. That's why I say adaptability is also being agile. You can be going full speed one direction, then you have to stop, turn around and do something completely different. You got to be agile, you gotta be quick on your feet. When it comes to things like that. That's just how the industry is as a whole. You have to be prepared for any and every inconvenience that could possibly go down. I believe it was Murphy's law, anything that can go wrong will, that is certainty in hospitality,

You find out who you are In those times and you find out how resilient you are, you find out how thick skinned you are, you find out how good you are at this industry. In those times, you find out more about yourself than you will, when things go right. It makes you a better person in the long run. So you have to be open minded about that, keep your cool and be level headed and, in all honesty, you have to appreciate those times. You can never technically predict when things will go wrong, you just have to anticipate it. You have to anticipate it and adapt. That is one of the big things a lot of people won't tell you about this industry. That's one of the dark sides of the industry, everything can change at a moment's notice. You can stop whatever you're doing, and go a completely different way.

Another great example of this is, we were scheduled to do an entire lunch buffet. For a super VIP group at one of the hotel restaurants I was working for. I mean it was pre made for at least 30/50 people. We received notice one hour before they arrived, they no longer wanted the buffet setup. They all wanted to order A la carte. That is so stressful. You start to think to yourself how inconsiderate, can someone be? Then you remember, This is the business of hospitality, things change very rapidly. Which is why I say that one of the biggest characteristics of a hospitality professional is to be adaptable.

Now you gotta find a solution. The client doesn't care what you have to do. But you have to make them happy, you have to make sure you're able to accommodate and you have to do it with a smile. No matter how frustrating it is, no matter how many hurdles you have to jump through. You have to make that happen. Whether you have to coordinate with different departments, or If you're not capable of accomplishing that goal in house. You have to outsource, you have to go to another restaurant, or you have to find another property but have to accommodate as best you can. Times like that will show you just what you are made of.

I learned to never come back without a solution you always have to provide options, and that is a part of being adaptable. Adaptability doesn't just mean, here's the solution. Many times you won't have the clear cut solution. You have to have several alternatives, and you have to bring that back to your client , guest, or boss. It'll be your bosses who will throw you these curveballs, and you have to just be able to go with it, roll with the punches. So you always want to bring back various solutions, different alternatives, that get the job done. It's not technically what was wanted, or what was demanded, but it did get the job done for sure.

So that's why there's a whole chapter on adaptability. I can't stress it enough. It's just that when things change, they change quickly. You have to be able to maneuver. You have to be able to change your course as quickly as possible, and then go full speed in the opposite direction. Sometimes you can anticipate it. A lot of times you can't.

I'll give one more example: I'm working overnight. As the front desk manager. And it's literally about three or four o'clock in the morning. I'm about to turn the day meaning I'm about to run the night audit. During that time my system shuts down and I can't check guests in or out. I can't get into the room's software program for at least an hour and a half, two hours while the system updates. I start the audit and I want to say, 30 minutes into my audit. An airline crew strolls in. And I'm not talking about some small airline. I'm talking about at least 50 people. 20/30 rooms. The pilot is paying with his corporate card. Now, I was only in this position for about four months at this point. I was responsible for everything. It definitely was a curveball because I didn't know how to create a separate account and or a separate folio to charge all the hotel rooms to the one card. If you ran the card too many times, it would end up declining because the company would think it was fraud. (Shout out to American Express for your fraud services.) That was something I had to learn and account for on the fly. I was able to get everybody into their rooms in a timely manner without too much hesitation. But when you're set on nobody else showing up for the night then, I turn the day, that lets me know okay cool I can relax. I can eat! Finally, I can do some paperwork in the back, but that completely threw my entire schedule off. Now I'm scurrying to figure out how I am about to check all of these people in plus get these payments. Thank God I was able to, you know, keep my wits about me. I was able to secure payment for a couple of the rooms. Some of the better rooms, you know the captain and co-captain, were able to get their rooms secured. I didn't know how to create a master account, which is usually what we have the accounting department for. I had to do an accounting job, which brings me back to chapter three, ***specialize and diversify***, learn everything that goes into your specialization.

Needless to say, I got the job done, everything was well, and the entire crew was out the next day, because of course, airline crews stay for less than 24 hours, maybe 18 hours in a spot while they rest up,and then head right back out. But those were just a couple of the stories of being able to adapt and stay ahead of the game in this industry, because these curveballs will come. If you don't know how to handle it. You're going to get hit. And it's not like you're going to get walked like in a game of baseball No! You're going to get hit and you're going to be out! These curveballs will take you out if you don't know how to handle it or if you don't know the right people to go to. especially if you don't know the right way to handle certain situations or provide alternatives. You gotta stay quick on your feet, be agile and be adaptable.

CHAPTER FIVE

Be of Service – Job Security

"The Best way to find yourself is to lose yourself in the service of others." - Gandhi

What I like to call job security (at least within hospitality). Is being of service. You have to be of service to your colleagues, your guests, your co-workers, your bosses. That is essentially why you are in the business, you are at the beck and call of other people. Don't get it twisted that is by no means you have to be somebody's bitch or to be somebody's flunkey, or that you have to take disrespect from anybody because you definitely want to have pride, you definitely should demand respect as long as you give it. Being of service is you going above and beyond, doing your job and doing your job very well. you will secure your job, you will have job security, because your reputation will speak for itself your work ethic will speak for itself. Your knowledge of your position, of what needs to be done, of your day to day operation will speak for itself, because you know how to play it and you know how to excel at it.

Let me break down four different sectors to secure your job, to make sure you always have a job, and to basically make it seem like you're indispensable. The first one I'm going to touch on is *"do your job and do it well"*, where you will call upon your knowledge and experience. Second, you're going to *"do what others won't,"* which is being refreshingly different and leading by example. So when other people will be like, "that's not my job," or things like that you'll be the one who is like let me do it because it's gonna help me in the long run. Thirdly, you're gonna *"make yourself an asset."* By doing all these things you're gonna make yourself indispensable. You're gonna make yourself needed by doing things that others won't you become the go to. When you are able to do a task and do it effectively with a great sense of pride that breeds job security. Then lastly, to wrap it up you want to *"leverage your connections"*. We all know a friend of a friend who got a job because of who they know, or their parents are involved in some type of executive board. That is leveraging your connections. That way you'll always have a job. You always continue to get a paycheck, you always have job security, because at the end of the day, who you know holds power.

Do your job and do it well

Without further ado, we're going to step into the first section of chapter five do your job and do it well. We talked about, in chapter three and four, specializing in your niche and diversifying and being adaptable. That's going to be your call to greatness, because you know your job at this point, you have obtained so many different experiences and you're able to pull from a vastness of knowledge now that you know different alternatives. You have the experience to know what works in certain situations and know what doesn't work in certain situations. You're able to formulate solutions quickly and effectively to get the job done. While also being adaptable and agile in your decision making.

Rule of thumb to position mastery is after being in your position six months you have learned your position then after a year you have mastered it. You will have experienced and learned just about every aspect of your position. You've pretty much seen every outcome, every experience, every possible scenario that could happen, will happen within that year. Call upon those experiences you have, even if what you initially did, did not work out. Now, you know what to do better next time. You now have a method and a plan to better handle those situations.

When you take pride in your work, you'll do something well. That's why you'll be recognized for it and you'll be praised for it and you'll be known as that person to get something done. You will be the one that when shit hits the fan, they will be able to call you. When you've been through it already you know how to handle situations, because you've been on that other side and you know what will work and what won't work. You will be seen as a master of your craft, you will be seen as confident and respected, because you know how this goes. you will be looked to for leadership, you'll be looked to for direction. That is the makings of a great hospitality professional. To be a leader. To be looked at as someone of authority, someone who knows the answers. Even if you don't know the answers, you're going to be able to find out how to do it and you're going to learn from it and you're going to add these experiences to your memory banks. So when the next time comes you're going to be fully capable of handling that situation. Use everything you have, pull from every experience, pull from other people's experiences, things that you've learned, this is the point when you want to bring everything out.

One time when I was sent to work at the W Austin on what we call "task force". There was a piece of advice I was given by my colleague (Shoutout Nick Sanchez) that was actually a confidence builder for me because I didn't realize how good of a job I would do. He said, "You already know what to do. Get here, and show them what you're made of. Do your job and do it so well, like I know you can. You know the answers, because you've been prepared, nobody can take those experiences away from you. So, call upon everything that you've learned, and use it because it's exactly the same thing. You're just in a different environment!"

Do what others won't

So, knowing your job and doing it well will help you vastly in the long run. Part of knowing your job and doing it well, is doing what others won't. A personal example I used to secure myself a nice position. Which was a position that I held for a long time because it presented the most growth. I prefered to do what others did not want to do. My colleagues despised closing, they despised working late nights, they despised being there in the middle of the action. They prefered to get there early, get there mid day, so they can leave early, go about their lives and do the boyfriend/girlfriend thing you know the socialite thing. I really enjoyed the rush, I enjoyed the problems, I enjoyed the different scenarios, the decisions that I had to make in the rush of the busiest moments of the night. I enjoyed that thoroughly. That solidified a place amongst my colleagues where nobody else wanted to do this. I stepped up and said " give it to me. I'll do it." That made me revered amongst my colleagues, my staff and my superiors. They looked at me as like, okay, you can handle these types of tasks and you can handle the toughest situations. At the end of the day, I was there to do a job, and I was there to do it very well. That segues to leading by example when you get to that point of management or leadership roles.

you. People who know your work, who know how well you do your job, how much of a leader you are, how valuable you are to a team, how much of an asset you are. Leveraging your connections to secure your job, gets you job security. I'm pretty sure as you read this, you know somebody who got a position because of someone they knew, that's leveraging your connections. Not meaning you won't be terminated you'll just be moved around if things go wrong.

It's always good to have friends in corporate positions. It's always good to have friends in high places because they will vouch for you, they will put their reputation on the line for you, and they have built up a network far beyond yours. If you're reading this, you're probably just starting out in the hospitality industry or hell you may be a veteran in the industry. It's always good to have friends, family, colleagues, mentors, in high places because you never know when you'll have to call on them. You never know when you have to use them as a reference. you never know how far their reach is.

So to recap on being of service, and securing your job. You have to do your job and do it well. Call upon your knowledge and your experience that you have gathered up until this point. Do what others won't, you have to be refreshingly different, you have to lead by example. They say the difference between leadership and management is leading by example. make yourself an asset, making yourself highly needed, make sure you are missed when

You have to lead by example for your staff for those who are under you, because they're going to come to you with a bunch of things that they don't want to do, and rightly so. Some of the tasks that they get asked to do, I wouldn't even want to do, but I sucked it up. I made an executive decision and said "you know what, I need you here, and I need you there. I need you to do this. I'm gonna go do this, so you can do what you have to do, focus on that and I'll go do this." That was leading by example, in my opinion, doing things that others hated, to get a job done because at the end of the day we're there to do a job, and that is to be of service.

Leading by example will be refreshingly different and will set you apart from your counterparts, and from others who may have had the same experiences or who may be even more qualified than you. Being called a leader who leads by example and not one to just bark orders will definitely set you apart from your counterparts. You will be looked upon favorably and regarded highly amongst your superiors. Do what others won't, be refreshingly different, and lead by example.

This will just make you an asset, meaning that it will hurt the operation to not have you. Creating your job security.

you're not there, and it definitely makes you valuable. then you leverage your connections. know somebody that knows somebody that knows somebody that can validate you, who can attest to your showmanship to your work ethic and to your accolades to your knowledge to your experiences. Those four things will secure your job. no matter how many times you move around. You will almost always be guaranteed a higher position or more perks if you know how to be highly sought after. Every time you move.

CHAPTER SIX

It's Who You Know

"The richest people in the world look for and build networks. Everyone else looks for a job." - Robert Kiyosaki

In the conclusion of chapter five. I brought up the topic of how having a solid network or people to vouch for you can supplement your need to be in certain experiences or certain positions, longer than you wish. This primarily pertains to executive positions, or management positions. Having people vouch for you is as good as gold. So that's why chapter six is about who you know. First find a mentor or several mentors. You need to get someone that has done what you want to do. Next, make connections with your colleagues, because there's been several times where I've been referred to fill a role from a colleague. I've been handed positions from past colleagues I used to work with. The opportunity might not have been right for them but they knew I would be perfect for the job. Then, you want to network, network, network. There have been countless times that I've met significantly powerful people that are not even in the hospitality industry but that are connected. If you dont network you'll never get to know them. So you have to network, network, network. Finally, you have to build genuine relationships, and this is referring to people in general because they can refer you to somebody just as easily as one of your colleagues or mentor.

Those are the four areas in networking to capitalize on, because the thing is who you know, and to keep your game tight. You got to cultivate these lasting and genuine relationships. I can use this person, might be the way you get an introduction, but you have to be genuine about it, you have to actually put effort into maintaining these relationships. It's like picking a realtor, when your business is flipping houses. You want to pick a realtor that you know you can go to, you have your favorite realtor, you have your favorite contractor, designer, architect, etc. You have these certain people that you know you can go to. It's the same principle that applies here. These people will put you on to deals or properties and in positions of opportunity that will be in your best interest and will ultimately benefit you in the long run. So you have to cultivate these genuine relationships with these four groups of people. Everybody needs a team, everybody needs support. Everybody needs help, everybody needs to be validated.

Find A mentor

Get you a mentor. I touched on mentorship in chapter two, when it comes to a form of education and experience, because a mentor, 9 times out of 10 has been in your position, and is substantially further ahead than you. A mentor can be someone you know, it can be someone you don't know, it can be someone you idolize, someone you look up to, a hero. having a mentor, if like having a personal trainer in the gym. They will coach and motivate you , but they will still let you take your own path. Having a mentor will make it easier for you during transitions on your journey. Not necessarily saying you have to follow their every move to the letter.

A mentor is a key component in advancing your hospitality career because they've been there. They've done it already. They know how the game is played, they know what it is to struggle to get into that position that you want. When you're just looking for a big break, they will tell you how they did it, they will tell you it wasn't easy but look here's a shortcut. Get you a mentor, someone you can trust. If you want to pull from your personal life or past bosses because they have years invested in the game they know how it's played and that's what you're looking for in a mentor. Someone who has the expertise, the knowledge, and who is accredited, then their network becomes your network.

Expanding your network, being broad in your reach and utilizing as many connections as possible will be extremely beneficial. You might be able to use one of those connections to help you in any situation. You have to be willing to be someone's mentee and when you choose a mentor, especially if it's someone you know, stay in contact. Relationships have to be nurtured, they have to be courted, they have to be genuine. You can't just say someone is going to be my mentor, and then you never speak to them for six months. It's like a friendship but on a professional level, because they're like a coach to you. They're going to help you make these plays and they're going to essentially help you and mold you into a better hospitality professional. That's all we want to do is be a better hospitality professional. Get you a mentor, learn from them as much as possible, hang out with them as much as possible, grab as much knowledge as you can, learn from their experiences. Heed their advice, heed their warnings, make those genuine connections, and be open minded to the experiences.

You'll realize they've been through every single thing that you're going through and it probably isn't as bad as you think. They're going to make light of the situation, but they're going to give you the exact motivation you need. They're not going to sugarcoat it though. They will share with you what you should do, then you go do it. Then you realize it wasn't as bad you thought. Thank them for their advice because they could have just as easily let you figure it out on your own, which is what a lot of people in this industry will do. Many people will definitely let you figure it out on your own. Sometimes they are not going to give you a shortcut because nobody gave them a shortcut. That's the difference between an old colleague or old boss and an actual mentor, a mentor is one that will show you the ropes. Go make those connections.

Being in this industry, you'll meet a lot of people. When I say, a lot of people I mean, a lot of people! When you go from property to property, you want to hold on to those connections. You want to hold on to those people that you meet because those experiences with those colleagues will leave lasting memories and lasting impressions. There's been plenty of times I've been offered several opportunities from people that I worked with. Whether it be, them not being available for the opportunity or they simply did not want to do it. They thought of you, because of the genuine connection, great experiences, and sweat equity that you guys put in together.

Make Connections

Make genuine friendships, make genuine connections and keep in contact with those who you work with. Especially if you're going from property to property or department to department, as you should be. Keep those connections, because you never know your connections might be able to help somebody else. A great example. I was thinking of switching roles from staying at a single property operation to being able to go to work out of several multiple properties. One of my colleagues (Shoutout Kirk Smith) had another colleague who was in that exact position that I wanted to be in. He put me in touch with his buddy and I was able to get the inside scoop of what that position was. He was able to share with me his stories and his wisdom, when it came to that position. So you want to keep those connections. Keep Up with folks and check in on them from time to time. If you're not at that property anymore or If you are at the property with them just build genuine friendships because it'll last longer. People in the hospitality industry hang with other people in the hospitality industry. It is not as small as you think, you'll realize a lot of your friends, a lot of your colleagues roll in the same circle of friends. You might be out catching a drink after work and end up finding a mutual friend at the bar and both of you know that same people, now you got another connection with this colleague. That's a bond. That's a genuine connection.

So you want to continue to harvest those connections. Every time you change a property. Every time you get a new position. Every time you're thinking of trying something different, reach out to your network. That leads to our third topic "network, network and network."

* Network, Network, Network*

Now when I say network, network, network that doesn't necessarily mean within your property or within your mentor aspect. That means, while you're on the job, while you're at seminars or classes. Outside of work, and sometimes at work as well. I've definitely made plenty of connections at work, from random people I interact with. They turned out to be great friends in the long one. We did great business together, it was a genuine connection. A lot of patrons would frequent my old establishments. These people worked in various parts of the corporation at different properties. They would frequent my property to have a drink, to have a meal. Doing your job and doing it well while meeting these people also expands your reach and network. you want to keep these people in your pocket, you want to keep these people aware of what you're capable of. Now you're building experiences, you're building memories. Now you're getting into that friendship stage. You made them look good in front of their bosses or family etc. It's easier for them to sell you to their boss because if their boss was there or if their other colleagues were there, they too have a reference point too, to attest to your skills. It's all about being validated.

Now you're validated in several groups within your industry. You gotta keep those people in your pocket, you gotta keep those people in your network, because you never know where that next opportunity will come from.

That just goes to staying on your toes. Always, always stay on your toes, that'll lead to opportunities. People can vouch for you when they know you can get the job done. Opportunities are just going to flow to you. Even if you have a good situation going in your current position. People will make a way for you to be able to move around.

If you do your job well enough. If you make the right connections. People will open doors for you. Essentially, you will open doors for yourself because you're the one who's cultivating these networks and these genuine relationships. So you got to keep networking. The bigger and better your network, the more opportunities you have.

Build Genuine Relationships

Last but not least, I suppose you know building genuine relationships. Now building genuine relationships ties all of this together. The moment someone sees that you're only befriending them or you're only doing your job just to get something out of them. You ruin the relationship. You've ruined that possibility of future engagements. It's like, I'm only doing what I need to be doing in front of you, to get something out of you. That's not genuine. That doesn't help anybody and it certainly doesn't help you. So you have to cultivate genuine relationships.

Genuine relationships will take you a hell of a lot further in life. When you build your relationships you have people you can call, you have people you can ask for advice, you have people you can invite places. You have better memories, better experiences, now you have better opportunities that just opened up for you. Meeting people through mutual friends within the industry that, technically you don't work with is the best form of marketing. Building relationships through word of mouth. So, you have to build these relationships because you never know where your next referral is gonna come from. It can be from someone you don't even work with. You could've just met them through somebody, while you were out at this thing. You told them what you do, and boom, now you have four or five leads in your pocket, just because you had a good time and you built a genuine relationship. You were able to cultivate it and make something shake from that connection. So build these relationships and make it count. Stay connected, check up on them every now and again. Invite them places, invite them to your establishment. You'll get invited to more places and you'll be able to reach more people, because that's what a network is. A network is a reach of people, especially in the hospitality industry, because the industry is so big and it covers so many different things. It will take you so much further, than you could imagine. You have to be able to build genuine relationships and meet as many people as you can. So build your relationships, network, network and network, make those connections and get you a mentor because it's who you know, and this will definitely keep your game tight. And I promise you you will go far when you do these things.

CHAPTER SEVEN

Keep Moving

"If you always put limits on everything you do, physical or anything else, it will spread into your work and into your life. There are no limits. There are only plateaus, and you must not stay there, you must go beyond them." - Bruce Lee

You made it this far, you might as well keep going. That is the whole premise behind this chapter to **Keep moving around**. You were able to harness these skills, you built a solid foundation, you learned these characteristics. You were able to find your niche and specialize in it, and you're able to adapt to your surroundings. You solidified your job security by being of service and you cultivated an outstanding network. Building a phenomenal career in hospitality in the process.

Depending on how hard you worked and how solid your foundation is now you have to move on. Be it relocation to another market or a different department or even a different sector of hospitality. Moving around was one of the biggest lessons that I had to learn in my entire career. I definitely failed this test on several occasions. Once I started to get into a property that I liked or I started to have fun. I lost sight of the goal. That's something that is hard to bounce back from you can't lose sight of the goal. You can't get complacent. Complacency leads to stagnation, stagnation breeds mediocrity. You never want to be mediocre in this industry, you never want to have a just getting by type of attitude. That might work in school. That might work in other jobs but not in this industry especially when you want to grow.

You don't want to be mediocre, you want to be the best, you want to be substantially better than the rest. You want to stand out from all your other counterparts, you want to have all the notoriety, you want to be revered amongst your colleagues as one of the greats to do it. With that, you have to keep moving. Never get too attached to a single location. Especially if you're young and you don't have any ties, you're not committed to anybody, you're not married, you don't have kids. You're living in an apartment where you have to renew your lease yearly. You don't have any obligations that will keep you cemented in the area that you are in. Move around!

The best advice I can give to you in achieving a prosperous, fulfilling hospitality career is to keep moving.

Always go to different properties. If you're so keen on a certain location, or area of the world, go! Find a way to make it happen, even if it is a temporary position. Experience something different. You cannot stay in a single place for too long. The rule of thumb is that to learn a position, you only need six months to a year. A year in a position means you have mastered that position. You've been in that position too long, you practically learned everything you can learn about that single position. Now it's time to move on to do something different. Now that year time frame is in reference to entry level non managerial positions. Management positions should be held for roughly at max two years and nothing more.

You have to keep adding skills, adding knowledge, adding connections, adding experiences, you have to keep adding to your portfolio, to your resume, to your experience bank to make the most out of this career. As I said in chapter four, this industry is always changing and you have to change with it. You can't have an upperhand on something that's changing, by staying the same. It just doesn't make sense and is not going to work for you.

Something I found that I wish I could have done was move around more. If you're in college and have access to internships I suggest taking this route. In your senior/junior year, secure one of those managerial internships that allows you to see several different departments, one of those year long internships. That's so you have working groundwork of managerial experience. If you're not in that internship yet you should follow this plan from the time you're a freshman to the time those internships come around. Take those 2 or 3 years to experience entry level positions. Stay in those positions for about 6 months each and then go do something else. By the time your internship comes around you will be so far ahead of all your counterparts you will be the perfect candidate due to being well rounded.

Touching back on chapter three, find your niche, find your specialization. Then you diversify. The goal while in college is to experience as much as you can. Your course load will show you the possibilities that hospitality has. What you do outside of classes should be is experiencing those things. No matter what you do, lay out a plan for yourself to experience the most.

When I was in undergrad, I worked at two properties and during my time there, and I held several positions. I did front desk operations, and I was in banquets, over the course of four years. I actually held every position you could. In banquets, I went from a banquet server, to banquet bartender, to lead server/bartender, and I filled in as banquet set up, rounding out my time in banquets as a banquet captain. You have to know everything about certain positions to know where you would like to fit, or what captures your attention, and all that does is just make you more valuable, make you more of an asset to your next position and you can throw that on your resume.

Being able to say, I have this experience. I was able to bartend, I'm able to serve, I know various serving techniques, I know about the beverage game, I can make different cocktails. I know how to lead a group, I have leadership experience. I know how to handle accountability because if something didn't get done, that was on me. I know how to send reports as a banquet captain. I know how to sit in meetings and take good notes, because I have pre shift meetings, or I have weekly event order meetings to go over what's coming for the next month or next week. Those are the types of things you have to plan out in your adventure in hospitality. A number of entry level positions to serve as your foundation providing you with a lot more knowledge than just staying in a single position for a year or two years.

To recap Develop a two year plan of varying departments and entry level positions. Once you build that solid ground, build upon that with direct leadership roles or skills. You want to start looking at management positions. Plus, by starting in college, by the time you hit your mid 30s, you can be in an upper management level or you can be at executive levels clearing a six-figure salary with full benefits. Think about it if you're 18 and a freshman in college. By the time you're 35, you would have spent 17 years in the industry. That is a lifetime, especially if you maneuvered properly. That is a literally a lifetime of experience that a lot of your superiors might not even have in hospitality. Your experience will be specifically in hospitality. Just think about all the different positions that you can have, all the different experiences that you can have in 17 years. You won't even be 40 years old and will already have nearly two decades in the industry.

How many people can say that at your age? Let's figure you devote four years to entry level positions. Then you finally decided to take it up a notch to management levels, and you invest another 10 years of management levels. You'll be 32! You're still really young, and then you go another four or five years and you still haven't touched 40 yet! At that point you should be well into upper management, the more senior levels where you make the big bucks. In hindsight, it won't seem that long and it won't seem that hard, because you're not even halfway through your life. And you're decades ahead of your superiors.

That brings me to the rotation of management positions and how long you should be in a given management position. Max management position should be held for two years with a minimum of a year. Figure that it'll take you a full year to see every season in that position, and everything that you could possibly experience within that year will happen. By the end of a year, you should know your position very well. So you figure you spend the next six months after that coasting and building your network. Now you want to start shopping around, you want to start seeing what else you can add to your repertoire. So you want to definitely start doing that at 16 months.

Now you have a solid background when it's time to look at different upper management job positions. The requirements on these positions are usually looking for experience. The only thing that would help you supplement 10 years of work experience is having people that can validate your expertise, people who can vouch for you. It's the only way to supplement the lack of years, people who have been able to witness your work and have been around you and seen you in action that can vouch for you. Which is why we discussed building a strong network in the previous chapter, It's about who you know.

Now you have added tremendous value to yourself and have left your impact all over the industry. You have to actually realize just what you're worth and what you bring to the table.

CHAPTER EIGHT

Raise The Stakes

"You never get what you deserve; only what you have the leverage to negotiate" - J. Rose

Leading up to this point, you're ready to move on, you're ready to bounce around, you solidified yourself in several different positions, and you're to a point where you're no longer getting hourly wages now you're salary. So this is the tricky part, but this is also the fun part. Negotiating deals. Like benefits, severances, salaries, vacations, holidays, relocation, things like that. At this point of your career you have to be really good at deals to get the most benefits for yourself. Now you're all in because you have a passion for hospitality and years invested and at the end of the day we have to make a living. We have bills to pay, we have student loans to pay back (unless you were fortunate enough to get a scholarship). We have to earn a living, unless you're fortunate enough to do this as a hobby or smart enough to get out of the rat race, and you have used your experiences to secure multiple streams of income but that's a whole different story.

Now we're going to get into this chapter on raising the stakes. Knowing your worth will be key. Keep pushing for more and know you are capable of more. Those are just pieces of advice. When you're browsing for new positions, or you're looking to relocate, getting into a new market and things like that. You have to remind yourself of those two things. Always know your worth, because nobody knows you're worth more than you and keep pushing for more whether it be knowledge, experience, or financial gain. Pushing for more won't allow you to settle. That's when you get complacent and that's when you start to stagnate. That's when you become mediocre and you no longer strive to be the best, you become like everybody else just trying to make ends meet. That's when you lose that passion, that's when you lose that drive. Always know that you are capable of more, as long as you keep learning, as long as you keep growing, as long as you keep gaining experiences, the more valuable you will be. But you have to want these experiences, you have to want to be better than you were the day before, the year before. You always have to be pushing yourself to be better than you currently are.

It's five main topics we're gonna cover in this chapter. First is know your worth and establish your bottom line. So when it comes to negotiations, those leadership positions and you're talking salaries, benefits, pensions etc. You have to set your bottom line. Your bottom line is the bare minimum that you will take. Secondly, you have to cater your resume to the position. Whoever said that you need a generic resume is a liar, and does not know what they're talking about. Every time you apply to a new position or you're looking to change positions, you have to cater your resume to make you stand out. I don't care if you apply for 100 different positions. That means you should have 100 uniquely different resumes, because for the most part, each position you apply for is going to call for a different set of skills that you have acquired up to this point. So, that's how you're going to stand out. They say rule of thumb, someone looks at your resume 20 seconds before deciding whether or not you're going to be a fit. So make unique resumes. Thirdly, you're going to use your resources, your network, and whatever you can to leverage beit skills, certifications, certificates, classes, seminars, your network of people or references. This is the point that you're going to use all of that. You're going to leverage everything you can, not only to meet your bottom line, but surpass your bottom line. That will be the difference between I got what I could and I got what I wanted. Use your leverage: you have to use your resources, and use your network. Let your network serve as validation and key information. Fourth you have to negotiate. Your negotiating skills have to be on point. When reaching that middle ground technically both sides lose, but it's not a big enough loss, where one side resents the other. So you have to make it fair, but you have to negotiate where you feel you're not being taken advantage of. Remember that most of the time when you're applying to these positions, these places have money. So, paying you is a drop in the bucket. So don't be afraid to negotiate strongly. Lastly, if they can't come to agreement with your terms that you feel is a great compromise or a great middle ground. Don't be afraid to walk away. When you know your value, you know your worth. You weigh the pros and the cons of the position, what you'll gain versus what you'll be losing. If it doesn't add up to your bottom line. You have to walk away, never feel pressured to take a position or devalue yourself into taking a position. That potentially will lead you to harm yourself in the long run.

Know your worth

So we want to get right into it. With, know your worth, and establish your bottom line. So at this point, you'd have built up an entire career, or at least half a career of groundwork of honing your skills building up experiences, gaining a plethora of knowledge to make you an asset in the hospitality industry, no matter where you go. Now you're at a point where you want to keep moving, you want to grow, you want to see different markets, you want to travel, which is a big part of hospitality, and you want to do different things. You have to remember how valuable you are, you have to remember what you bring to the table.

There will be a lot of other candidates, there will be a lot of other people applying for the same position, but you have to remember there's nobody like you on this earth. You are literally one of one, and that is what makes you unique. Nobody thinks like you, nobody will execute the way that you do, and nobody will have the exact same experiences that you do. That will be what sets you apart. Recall what you went through to get to this point. Remember the struggle, remember the blood, sweat and tears. Remember the nights that you put in overtime, the days when you went without sleep, the guests that you dealt with, the managers you had to deal with. The different people day in and day out that you dealt with. Think about the fact that you might have been working for less than you're worth, up until this point. That's just on the professional side.

Think of the personal side, if you have a family to take care of. If you have bills to pay like substantial recurring bills remember, these things come into play. When you establish your bottom line, you reevaluate your worth. If they can meet what you need, take it, but never start with your bottom line. We'll get to that in the negotiation section, but your bottom line is your bare minimum of what you'll take.

Say you apply for a position. When you apply, always have a number especially when you're jumping from position to position. You want to have a preset increase in mind, some places say 15% is a good increase, some will say 20%, some will have an actual dollar amount and won't do a percentage based off your previous salary or your previous hourly rate wage. You want to go in with a solid dollar amount based on what you feel like you're worth, and what you know you could bring to the table.

A colleague of mine said that he takes no less than a $7,500 increase whenever he changes positions. If he didn't know his worth, if he didn't know how valuable he was, he'd be willing to take anything just because the position sounds good. When you establish your bottom line, you establish your worth, you set a precedent for everybody and you stick to it. You have to hold yourself to it, don't fold from it, don't bend from it. There's always ways to make a deal more lucrative where everybody comes off a winner. But you have to establish that bottom line. That bottom line is what sets you apart from a person who took the job, and a person who was the best fit for the job. So establishing your bottom line is the first part of raising the stakes.

Cater you resume

Next you want to cater your resume. Now you can do this on your own, you can do this through a resume builder, or you can do this through a freelance resume professional. There's a lot of businesses out there who specifically build resumes to get you the most attention to make you stand out. They will highlight specific traits that are catered to the position in which you're applying. The days of having a standard resume, for every job position that you apply for are over. Your resume has to stand out above everybody else's. The way you set yourself apart is by highlighting the traits that they are looking for.

Notice when you go to apply for a position, they will list the requirements, and what you need to have in order to be a fit for that position, lead with those attributes to establish that you are well qualified for this position. If you don't meet those qualifications for the position, then highlight some profound traits that set you apart. It says , here are the things that I actually did that will set me apart from any other candidates.

You should always have multiple resumes on hand. I don't care how many you have, but you should definitely have multiple resumes they should always be changing, and every time you get a new position, update your resume. I know that to have multiple resumes is a lot, but you have to cater it to each job position. To make it easier, have a template resume. That way you don't have to keep doing the work over and over again. That will save you a lot of time, and that is working smarter not harder. When you already have your resume, written and drafted then all you have to do is edit.

Use your resources

Know your bottom line, then cater your resume to the position. Now you want to use your resources and your network. Use it as leverage. All of the experiences, all of the people you have met, the friendships you have made, the relationships you have established, grown and nurtured will play a key part for your resources. Knowing somebody, that knows somebody, that knows somebody, that knows you. Is a great way to leverage. Being local is something that you can leverage into a better position, or knowing people at a property. Leveraging your education, your alma mater, or your organization, fraternity, sorority etc. Leverage past experiences or classes you have taken. Leverage gives you the upper hand. at the end of the day you could always leave. You could always walk away. You could always say you know what, you don't see my worth. Sorry I'm gonna pass, because there will always be another job. There will always be another position, no matter how bad you want the position. There will always be another one and there will always be a better one. If they can't understand how valuable you are, then on to the next one. But you gotta use all your resources. Use all your network. Use all your leverage that you can to garner yourself a better deal, and to meet your bottom line, if not surpass it. Now you're really in the game now.

Negotiate

Now you're at the table. You know you're a perfect fit. They think you're a great candidate. Now let's talk turkey. This is the point where we're talking numbers. Now we're talking packages. Now we're talking benefits. This is where your negotiating skills come into play. You have to negotiate, negotiate, negotiate and negotiate hard!

When I was shopping around from going corporate to, you know, an independent business. A great piece of advice that was given to me was, factor in that you're not getting the same benefits anymore, factor in that you're no longer corporate and you know your salary won't be the same anymore. Factor that in, and you go up on your bottom line. You have to cover that spread. (Shoutout Chef Sam Santos) So you have to negotiate those things. When it comes to certain situations like that, that was a substantial piece of information from a friend of mine, a great colleague, and an excellent chef. It's a different ballpark out there. It's not corporate anymore, so you have the grounds to ask for substantially more to cover your medical expenses, your benefits, health packages, etc.

You have to negotiate hard, and when you start negotiating, it's a back and forth thing. It's a game. Sort of like playing tennis or ping pong. They send you an initial offer. You send your initial counter offer and make it high so there is room between them and your bottom line in your favor. Then they will hit you with a counter that you might not like. Then you start with incentives to sweeten the pot. So, if this is the price they're at? If you're not going to give me this, then I need this to supplement. Okay, we're not going to give you that, but we can give you this and supplement you here with that. There's a lot of things you can throw in to make the deal work for you. But you have to remember, If someone loses in the negotiating process that builds resentment and resentment leads to conflict later on down the road.

You have to set that bottom line, you have to set it aggressively, and never settle. Hennessy has a great slogan. "Never stop, never settle." Never settle, and start high in negotiations then work your way down, but never go below your bottom line. Never get greedy either. If you're able to walk away with your worth intact, and your needs met, great job. You've won already. Don't get greedy because greed will kill deals. When you think about it that's all this is when it comes to negotiating. It is a deal. You are working a deal to make sure that everybody comes out on top or everybody comes out happy and satisfied. There might not be winners, but you have to make sure that your needs are going to be met. Don't put yourself in a financial bind, don't put yourself in a mental construct, and don't hinder your growth. You should be able to have some flexibility and be able to negotiate on salary or in terms, because it's all about what you view as valuable when it comes to your negotiations.

Leave the table

In some situations they won't see your value, they won't see your worth, and they can't meet your bottom line. Last thing you can do is walk away. You will never lose yourself by walking away from a deal or from negotiations where they did not meet your bottom line. They failed to see your worth and your value, no matter who vouched for you, no matter who leveraged for you. If they fail to meet your bottom line. You have to walk away. Like, don't be afraid to walk away. Actually, it establishes the fact that you know you're valuable. In fact, I have another story.

I was put on to a position by a mentor of mine.(Shoutout Andrea) She thought I would be a great fit because she knew I was looking for something new and she was not available to accept the position. Now this position would have propelled my career. It was a general manager position and I would actually be running two separate venues. I met the owner and toured the venues and was excited to start a new endeavour. Once it came down to the compensation and duties that's when things started to get shaky. I would be required to work 6 days a week ,14hr days, while getting a brand new venue open and running an already open venue. There were no benefits, and the salary was 60k. This was a contingent six month deal, and at the end of six months I would renegotiate with the owner. The kicker was that I would start a week from signing the agreement letter. I was very hesitant about agreeing, something did not feel right about the deal. I was getting reemed, when it came to workload versus compensation. I ultimately had to turn down the position. A few months passed and I heard about the troubles the venues were having and how the GM that was hired in place of me had already quit, due to the same issues that I was able to notice. That could have easily been me, but I was not afraid to walk away, because I was losing on that deal, substantially.

Stick to your guns. Even if you have to walk away, establish your value. It shows that you know how to negotiate and it shows that you won't settle for anything less than your worth, especially after you executed everything in this chapter. Establish your worth and set your bottom line. You cater your resume, use your resources, your network and you leverage all of it to the best of your ability. Then you negotiate. Then if you can't come to some mutual agreement, walk away. You will be respected more, and you continue to hold fast to what you're worth. At the end of the day, they have to respect you. It's going to bite them in the ass because they should have definitely picked you, because you are the type of candidate that they need. Respect goes a long way in this industry, and it will open a lot of doors for you.

You have to play the game and you have to raise the stakes. Come to the table with all your ducks in a row. It's like playing spades, it's like playing poker. Only you know the cards you have in your hand. You have to know how to play them. You have to know how to use them. You have to know when to fold, when to call, and you have to know when your opponent is bluffing. You have to know when a deal is bad, you have to know what is no longer worth your time. But in the light of everything when you're able to make that negotiation. When you're able to make that compromise when you're able to meet your bottom line. Take it! Take it and run with it. Because as I said in the previous chapter. You gotta keep moving and make your next move your better move.

CHAPTER NINE

Remember your Why

"The real joy in life comes from finding your true purpose and aligning it with what you do every single day." - Tony Robbins

If you made it to the end of this book.I really appreciate you for sticking with me, I appreciate you for making it this far. If you correlate this book to your hospitality career. Get everything you can get out of it, all the experiences, the knowledge, the connections, the friends ,the good memories, the bad memories, the ups and downs, the life lessons, the financial lessons. You won't believe the places this industry will take you. You know you did amazing things, when you can look back and it was completely worth it.

If you go back to chapter one, find your why. To bring everything full circle chapter nine is about never forgetting your why. You have to tie it all together. In the end you have to remember what motivated you to start in the first place, because in this next step, you will step out on your own. Especially if you're looking for, you know that big impact. That big dare to be different. You have to step out on your own, you have to get out from under the shadow of Big Brother. If you did it right, if you did good business you made the right connections. At this point you have countless experiences good and bad. You now have everything you need, including resources and knowledge to set out on your own, and then build something for yourself.

Yes, you can do 25 years for a company and hit those milestones where you get benefits for life. At that point, your kids have graduated high school and are about to enter college. Coming full circle from when you started. Now you have the freedom, you have time, you have clarity of vision and you're only halfway there through your life. Now you can build something for your family. Now you can build something for your legacy. Build something for your kids, kids. Build something that will live on longer than you. Something that touches back to your "why".

Why did you start in the first place? Why did you get into this industry? Now, you use that to touch the masses on your own terms. Use that to build something of your own, use that why to make something that is lasting and something that keeps giving constantly. The moment you leave that company is when you can start making a real difference. Now it will be your turn to be a mentor to the next generation. You can be someone who the younger generation can call upon for references and things like that. Now you're the one who is credible, you are the one who can validate the work of others. At this point you know how to build something from the ground up, because you built a solid foundation.

You establish your why in the beginning, you build upon these key attributes. You never settled. You moved around, you were able to expose yourself to a variety of different experiences, cultures, different markets, you specialize and diversified yourself in your niche. Now take everything that you learned, compile it into one cluster, then give it to the world. Under your own power, on your own terms, or your own circumstances. At this point, you're super established, and that's the only way you can go up from this point. unless you're like, CEO or CFO or one of those super executive positions. People tend to hold those positions for you know 10/15 years. Even then you can still have a greater impact.

In building something you'll be able to give it to your kids,you'll be able to pass it down. Not only that, you'll be building generational wealth. So keep that in mind, when you bring everything full circle. It's the circle of Life. Ashes to ashes, dust the dust and some point we all have to leave this earth. You might as well leave behind something worthwhile. That's how you have to look at it, you started with your "why" and you're gonna end with your "why."

Much like this book started with finding your "why" your story will end with your "why".

When you end with your "why" you have to end it on your terms. You started embarking on a journey of 10,000 miles when you found your "why". That was the first step. Now that you completed this journey you look ahead in your life. At this point you're 50/ 60. Now you're looking at what's next? You're too young to retire. Retirement is not an option for you. So was what's next? What's the next journey in life? What's the next ride? Remember your "why". Have you accomplished what you set out to do? What will you do now to fulfill your purpose? If you just up and one day decide to stop living your purpose. You will feel worthless. Do something where you can still fulfill your purpose. It doesn't have to be grand. It doesn't have to be something outlandish. The saying goes, aim for the moon, and if you miss you'll land in the stars. You still end up out of this world, you still end up way further than you could have anticipated by setting your goal high. Set your goals substantially high so no matter where you land. It is better than where you started.

If your "why" is strong enough. Your "why" will be passed down from generation to generation. Ultimately, from the other side you will realize that your "why" carried on with you not being there. You will see your dream come to fruition, you will see everything that you've dreamed of come to pass in the lives of your children in the lives of your children's children. So, with that. Remember your why. Remember your purpose, remember why you started, because it got you to this point. And it's going to continue to take you further.

Use every chapter in this book, every piece of information, every piece of knowledge, every connection. Every experience that you gained to embark on the next set of endeavors or the next journey, because the sky's the limit. Honestly the sky isn't the limit, you can take it further than your wildest dreams. You just have to keep going. You have to remember your why. And bring it full circle. Then pass on the knowledge in the process. That is a "why" of mine. To pass on the knowledge that I've acquired from the experiences that I've gained and things that I went through to the next generations. So that it will be easier for them and they will be further ahead of the game than when I was starting out. We're all just trying to find our place in this world. We're all just trying to find where we fit in. We're all just trying to find our niche. once you find your "why" passing the information along it's kind of like paying it forward.

So, pay it forward, pass on the knowledge, pass on your wealth of knowledge, be that person that we talked about in chapter two, where the experience of others can be the foundation for somebody else for the next generation. Be that person in chapter six, be a mentor, be somebody's connection, be a part of somebody's network, build that genuine relationship. I will never say it enough because I need it to resonate with you that's why chapter nine is titled **Never forget your "Why"**. Always remember why you started.

Closing Remarks

I would like to thank you, for making it to the end of the book. Thank you to everybody that sat down to read this, as I said, in the opening. I want this book to be used as a tool for the next generation and generations to come. This can be used as a map or as a goto plan to help those who don't know which way to go, who don't know how to navigate this industry.

I wish that I had somebody or I was able to ask somebody to lay it out for me in this manner. A manner in which I was able to receive it. Because this industry is definitely a fun one. It's amazingly fun. You'll have great experiences, you'll meet a lot of people, but it's very difficult to navigate. Without the help of others without knowing somebody, and without a mentor, you will just be flailing around like a fish out of water, trying to get into the next pond.

I tried to be the light that I wish I had when I was coming up while I was doing my time in this industry. I wanted to fill the void, and I hope that, for those who read this, that void has been filled. I hope that this brings you a sense of direction. I hope this brings you some type of clarity and helps you fulfill your purpose and helps you understand how this industry maneuvers. I hope this allows you to, you know, get to wherever you wish to be.

You can take this industry as far as you want because the sky's the limit with this industry, this industry has so many possibilities and so many opportunities and it will literally take you any and everywhere that you can think of. All you have to do is be open, know how to move, know how to navigate and enjoy it. Enjoy the ride. That is the best thing I can say, enjoy the ride because it's not going to be all brunches and VIP sections. It is full of long nights, and even longer days. There's going to be bad experiences. But it's going to be amazing memories, and it's going to be a bunch of assholes that are going to test you in every single way possible. But you have to keep going, you have to remember why you're doing it.

Have fun. I hope this helps. I hope that you make a great name for yourself. And I hope that your "Why" is passed on from generation to generation. I hope you become a powerful asset in this hospitality industry. And I wish you nothing but the best of luck.

Oh!

YOU'RE F*CKING WELCOME

Love,

Jay Syrah

Acknowledgements

There is a list of talented individuals, family and friends I would like to thank! Without their help, guidance and experiences this book would not be possible. I am going to try my best not to forget anyone, but there are a lot of people to thank. First and foremost I would like to thank God almighty for setting my purpose and aligning all these great people and experiences in my path. My Parents and sister for giving me the right encouragement when I needed it and believing in me (sometimes). My long time friend Desia for helping me put a name to the industry that I longed to be a part of for so long. To my first hospitality professor at the College of Southern Maryland Prof. Bill Williams. To all the professors that I have had the pleasure of sitting in classes at UNCG. To Mrs. Cassandra Brown for being my first foot in the hospitality industry and looking after me like I was her own child, All my friends and colleagues at Quaintance Weaver Restaurants and Hotels. To my W DC Family; Chef Samual Santos, Chef Fabrizio Bueno, Andrea Cathy, Nick Sanchez, Abdul Raoof Hamidullah, Louis Galofre, Andrian Mishek, Andrew Seifers, Queenie Hoang, Lashawndra Jackson, Colby Carlton, Bradley Moore, Bradley Joseph, Anthony Berry, Nick Scherer, Kirk Smith, and so many others across the entire property (Talent included). To all of my colleagues and friends I have gained over the years (Shoutout Everyone at the Ritz Carlton Naples Golf Resort) thank you for sharing your stories and the memories. To all the DJ's I have had the pleasure of working with; Farrah Flosscett, DJ OZ, DJ Cory T, DJ Phlipz, DJ Eddo, DJ Kam, DJ EPX, DJ T Nyce, LexisLane, AlexLove, DJ RI5E, DJ Heat, Cheickmeout, DJ CYD and all of my nightlife connoisseurs that showed me the under belly of this amazing industry. If for some reason I forgot to mention you by name, by no means does that take away from the experiences we've had and the memories we've created!

Thank you all!!!

www.ingramcontent.com/pod-product-compliance
Lightning Source LLC
Chambersburg PA
CBHW011319080526
44589CB00018B/2735